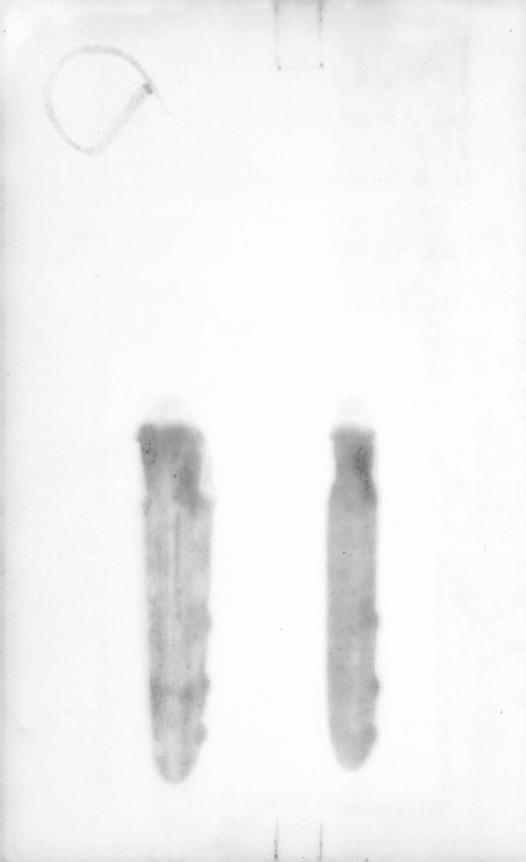

AMERICAN INDIAN HABITATS

American Indian
HABITATS

*How to Make Dwellings and
Shelters
with Natural Materials*

Nancy Simon
and
Evelyn Wolfson

Drawings and diagrams by Nancy Poydar

**David McKay Company, Inc.
New York**

Library of Congress Cataloging in Publication Data
Simon, Nancy.
American Indian habitats.
Bibliography: p. 97
Includes index.

SUMMARY: Describes natural materials and construction methods used for the
dwellings of eight native American culture areas and provides instructions for
making replicas of these shelters.
1. Indians of North America—Dwellings. [1. Indians of North
America—Dwellings. 2. Handicraft] I. Wolfson, Evelyn, joint author. II. Poydar,
Nancy. III. Title.

E98.D9S55   728   78-4416
ISBN 0-679-20500-4

1 2 3 4 5 6 7 8 9 10

Manufactured in the United States of America

Illustration Credits

Jean Alley, page 42; Kathy Erny, page 75; Fruitlands Museum, Harvard,
Mass., George M. Cushing, page 57, Paul J. Weber, page 84; *The Paper,*
Info-Media, Inc., page 95; Peabody Museum, Harvard University, Hillel
Burger, pages 27, 31, 45, 46, 60 (bottom), 87; Smithsonian Institution
National Anthropological Archives, pages 10, 32, 73, 86, John K. Hillers,
pages 26, 29, H. L. Hime, page 85, also published in David L. Bushnell, Jr.,
"Villages of the Algonquian, Siouan, and Caddoan Tribes West of the Missis-
sippi," *B. A. E. Bulletin 77,* Washington, D.C., 1922, William H. Jackson,
page 61, Frank A. Robinson, page 76, William S. Soule, pages 58, 72; South-
west Museum, Los Angeles, pages 5, 6, photo by Dickason, page 4; U. S.
Forest Service, page 48; *Wayland Town Crier,* Wayland, Mass. page 96.
Chapter spots by Marie and Nils Ostberg

THANKS

most of all to our husbands

Bennett Simon
and
Bill Wolfson

to our children
Jonathan and Amy Simon
and
Jason and Dacia Wolfson

to
Elaine Dohan

to
Dr. Jeffrey Brain, Curator,
Peabody Museum, Harvard University

for photographs
Kathy Erny, Jean Alley, and Rita Anderson

to
The Elbanobscot Environmental Education Center,
and all those associated with it, who introduced
us to the world of the American Indian

and to the many students
who helped us build Indian dwellings.

CONTENTS

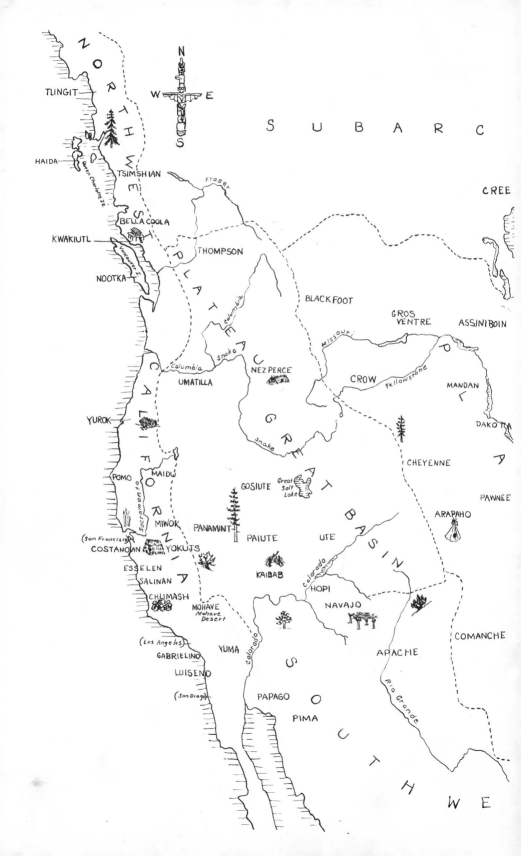

Map shows 12 botanical references, 11 different dwellings, the tribes mentioned in the text, and 6 of the major geographic divisions of the North American Indians.

MONTAGNAIS - NASKAPI

T I C

MICMAC

MALECITE

ABENAKI

OJIBWA (CHIPPEWA)

Lake Superior

OTTAWA

HURON

MENOMINI

Lake Huron

Lake Ontario

MOHAWK

SAUK

NEUTRAL

IROQUOIS

SENECA

CAYUGA

ONEIDA

FOX

Lake Michigan

ONONDAGA

POTAWATOMI

Lake Erie

SUSQUEHANNA

KICKAPOO

ERIE

Missouri

MIAMI

ILLINOIS

O R T H E

S T

SHAWNEE

CHEROKEE

S

KIOWA

CATAWBA

Z

OSAGE

CHICKASAW

Mississippi

A

E

MUSKOGEE (CREEK)

G

CADDO

T

H

CHOCTAW

NATCHEZ

O

S

TIMUCUA

S

SEMINOLE

S T

Nancy Poydar

MAJOR TRIBES OF NORTH AMERICA

California-Northwest

Bella Bella
Bella Coola
Chinook
Chumash
Costanoan
Esselen
Gabrielino
Haida
Hupa
Karok
Klamath
Kwakiutl
Luiseño
Maidu
Miwok
Modoc
Mohave
Nootka
Pomo
Quinault
Salish
Salinan
Tlingit
Tsimshian
Wintun
Yokut
Yuma
Yurok

Great Basin-Plateau

Bannock
Cayuse
Flathead
Goshute
Kaibab
Nez Percé
Paiute
Panamint
Shoshone

Shuswap
Thompson
Umatilla
Ute
Washo
Yakima

Southwest

Acoma
Apache
Havasupai
Hopi
Jemez
Jicarilla
Maricopa
Navajo
Papago
Pima
Pueblo
Walapai
Zuñi

Plains

Arapaho
Arikara
Assiniboin
Blackfoot
Cheyenne
Comanche
Crow
Dakota
Gros Ventre
Iowa
Kansa
Kiowa

Mandan
Missouri
Osage
Oto
Pawnee
Quapaw
Santee
Sioux
Wichita
Yanktonnai

Southeast

Apalachee
Atakapa
Caddo
Catawba
Cherokee
Chickasaw
Chitimacha
Choctaw
Creek
Natchez
Pensacola
Powhatan
Seminole
Timucua
Tamathli
Tuscarora
Yuchi

Northeast

Abnaki
Algonkian
Beothuk
Cayuga

Chippewa
Delaware
Erie
Fox
Huron
Illinois
Iroquois
Kickapoo
Malecite
Massachusetts
Menomini
Miami
Micmac
Mohawk
Mohican
Montauk
Narragansett
Neutral
Ojibwa
Oneida
Onondaga
Ottawa
Passamaquoddy
Pennacook
Penobscot
Peoria
Pequot
Piankashaw
Potawatomi
Prairie
Sauk
Shawnee
Seneca
Susquehanna
Wampanoag
Winnebago

INTRODUCTION

A squirrel hauls leaves high in a tree to build a large summer nest. In winter he moves into a hollow log. People have also looked to nature for places to live and for materials to build their homes. The first inhabitants of North America, the North American Indians, used the trees of the forests, the plants of the meadows and marshes, the stones, muds, clays, and sod of the earth, and the hides of animals to build their practical dwellings. These dwellings reflected the strong relationship between the Indians and their environment.

How these dwellings were built and which materials were used in their construction is relatively simple to determine. Why each tribe chose to build a particular kind of dwelling is not so easy to determine.

If we want to know why certain materials were used to build a home, we must first learn something about the availability of the materials in a particular environment. We also must know something about the geography and climate of the area. For example, the coastal mountains along the Pacific Northwest extend all the way to the sea. The Japan Current brings warm moisture in from the Pacific and creates a very mild land climate for a northern latitude. Because the conifer forests of the Northwest thrive on a combination of heavy precipitation and mild temperatures, it's not surprising that the Indians of the area used conifer trees to build their homes.

There are also areas where mountains have caused deserts. The Sierra Nevadas in California form a moisture barrier that creates deserts in the valleys west of the mountains. Because of this condition, there is little vegetation in the area, and few Indians made their homes there.

Geography and climate can also affect the choices of dwellings and building materials in other ways. The Central Plains were once covered with short and tall grasses, yet all the Plains Indians did not cover their dwellings with grass. Prior to the introduction of the horse by the Spanish explorers, most tribes lived on the fringes of the Central Plains, and hunted relatively short distances on foot. The tribes who eventually followed the migrating herds of buffalo designed and built the tipi, a lightweight, portable structure suited to a migratory way of life. Grazing buffalo fed on the grasses of the Plains, and buffalo hides became the material most readily available to the Indians for home-building.

Another aspect of the environment which was important to the Indians (although its importance is less obvious to us) was the availability of food sources. North American Indians were farmers, fishermen, hunters, and wild-food gatherers. Some were more specialized in one of these areas than others. Why the Indians built a particular dwelling out of a particular material often depended on how they obtained their food.

xiv

The Indians of the Plains are also a good example of how certain lifestyles affected home-building. Because the Plains Indians had to move with the migrating herds of buffalo, they did not build large, permanent dwellings. However, severe weather conditions required warm shelters in winter that would protect them from the cold and strong winds. In terms of comfort, the tipis were as warm and well-built as the permanent dwellings of Indians in other regions. And they were often just as large, since the Plains tribes took their entire families with them when they traveled. Was this because the skills needed to prepare the hide, bones, horn, and sinew of the buffalo for a myriad of uses belonged exclusively to the tribal women? Or was it because the women were customarily responsible for home-building? The tradition of who built the dwelling—the men or the women—was a very important consideration.

Other tribal traditions also influenced the design of Indian homes. The Pueblo of the Southwest lived in large, geometric stone-and-adobe dwellings. Yet, when the Navajo came to the Southwest, they built a very different, round-shaped dwelling. Some anthropologists believe that the Navajo originally lived in the north, and that the tribe adhered to the northern tradition of building rounded homes.

In order to further understand the practicality of Indian homes, we must also understand something of Indian beliefs about how they should live in relation to both people and nature. Compared to our modern society, the Indians had a much keener sense of the advantages of communal and cooperative living. This was partly due to necessity. Survival often depended on communal efforts to obtain and store food. But cultural attitudes also played important roles. Native Americans felt a kinship with the natural world. Members of the Mandan tribe, for example, believed they sprang from the earth in a particularly fertile spot near the Missouri River. The Sioux believed that everything in life was related to a circle. Because the birds made circular nests, the tribe built circular tipis. The

Kaibab Indians of the Great Basin used the overhanging limbs of live trees for the frames of their dwellings. This was not just an ingenious idea created out of necessity, it also reflected a knowledge and appreciation of the natural materials in their environment.

By observing and experimenting with some of the materials Indians used to build their homes and shelters, we can appreciate the ingenuity of America's first inhabitants. We can also better appreciate the skills and materials needed to create our own comfortable, modern-day homes.

At the end of the book, you will find a table of common metric conversions and equivalents; at the end of each chapter is a section on how to make a replica of an Indian dwelling or shelter.

AMERICAN INDIAN HABITATS

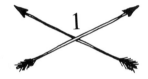

CALIFORNIA-NORTHWEST

From the deserts of southern California to the Canadian subarctic region of the northwest, European explorers found many large and small Indian villages. The dwellings ranged from simple brush shelters in the south to large, wood-plank houses in the north.

The California Indians built small, permanent settlements in the deserts, in the foothills of the Sierra Nevadas, in the valleys, and along the coastal plain. The amount and variety of food sources were vast. The tribes hunted throughout the year, and fished and gathered plants and berries in season. As soon as one food supply diminished, another became available. This abundance of food allowed generations of California Indians to live solely off the land, without ever having to farm it.

An exception to this was the Yuma tribe of the Mohave Desert. The tribe obtained some of their food by gathering pinyon pine nuts and mesquite. They could not, however, exist on what they gathered. Instead, they emulated the Pueblo and other neighbors in the southwest and planted corn, squash, beans, and pumpkins. These gardens supplied them with more than half of their food.

The Yuma built log-and-pole-framed dwellings, thatched with arrow weeds and covered with sand. Because of frequent cold winds from the north, the doors always faced south. Yuma dwellings resembled the Navajo hogan of the southwest.

The Yokut Indians onced lived in the San Joaquin Valley and among the southern foothills of California's Sierra Nevadas. In early times, the Kern River drained into a large shallow basin, now known as Tulare Lake. The tule swamp, which originally surrounded the lake, has since been reclaimed and cultivated. Tule is a bulrush, which was collected by the Indians in October. The leaves were then dried and woven into strong, waterproof mats.

The steep, gable-roofed dwellings of the Yokut were often covered with tule mats. These were made by sewing each leaf together with a bone needle and thread made of tule fibers. Yokut dwellings, which often housed as many as ten families, usually had shade porches.

Yokut dwelling.

An indispensable Yokut shelter, used during the hot California summers, was the *ch'iniu,* a flat tule-covered roof supported by posts. The Yokut also enjoyed bathing in small sweathouses, which they dug in the earth, framed with posts, and covered with mud.

In the shadows of the Big Tree *(Sequoia gigantea),* along the northern foothills and valleys of the Sierra Nevadas, lived the Maidu, Miwok, and northern Yokut tribes. They built their homes in the narrow canyons and valleys along the tributaries of the Sacramento River, where the climate is mild and moist.

The Maidu built multi-family, earth-covered dwellings, called *hübos.* Hübos were dug in the earth at a depth of three feet below ground level. The pits were framed with pinyon pine timbers, then covered with earth. In summer, the Maidu moved outdoors, where the tribe cooked, ate, and slept. Sometimes they built temporary, cone-shaped homes, each ten to fifteen feet in diameter. Several poles were leaned together and tied at the top. A shallow excavation was made in the earth to form the floor. The bark of dead trees, pine needles, and an assortment of sticks and brush were used for floor covering.

Many clans of the tribe occupied the area known today as Yosemite Park. There, among the giant Sequoia trees, grew

Maidu temporary summer shelter.

Miwok house frame.

sugar pines and incense cedar. The bark of the incense cedar was used by the Miwok to cover a cone-shaped dwelling, framed with long, thin poles.

Along the coast of California, between San Francisco and San Diego, is a shallow plain with a climate distinctly different from the rest of the state. Rain occurs in the late fall and winter, and temperatures rarely drop to freezing. Nights along the coast are cool, and there is often early morning fog. The Costanoan, Esselen, Luiseño, Salinan, Chumash, and Gabrielino tribes once lived in this area. These clans enjoyed coastal and deep-sea fishing and shellfish gathering. Some of the tribes built large, hemisphere-shaped dwellings which held as many as fifty people. The houses were framed with willow or live oak saplings. Additional saplings were placed around the houses' circumferences and covered with tules. Earth was then placed around the bottoms of the outer walls for added support and protection from drafts.

The Chumash Indians were one of the few California groups to use beds. The beds were raised off the ground and placed around the inside perimeters of the dwellings. Tule mats covered the beds and were rolled up for pillows.

North of San Francisco is an area with high cliffs that overlooks a rock-bound coast and the sea, where steady winds blow most of the time. The region has no natural harbors, but in the

Construction of typical southern California brush hut.

Chumash dwelling, tule mats at left.

areas where several rivers flow into the Pacific, the Pomo Indians once established their small settlements. In summer, the tribe hunted sea lions and gathered mussels. In spring, salmon were plentiful. The nearby forests of giant redwoods were not exploited by the Pomo because few animals lived there.

Almost one-third of the Pomo tribe settled along the banks of what is now called Russian River, a stream which flowed through several small valleys on its course to the ocean. The Pomo erected two types of dwellings along the Russian River. One type had a framework of poles (often consisting of white oak saplings) bent together at the top and tied. These were thatched with bundles of grass, attached to the horizontal poles of the frame and clamped down with an additional pole.

Around Clear Lake, the largest fresh-water lake in California and located forty miles north of what is now the city of Santa Rosa, Pomo dwellings were elliptical, and covered with tule instead of grass.

The northernmost settlements of California belonged to the Yurok tribe, who made use of the region's dense redwood forest. European explorers were amazed to find huge, redwood-plank houses along this section of the Pacific coast. The houses were made of planks, placed horizontally or vertically on top of massive frameworks of timbers.

A Yurok plank house was constructed on two levels. One-half of the diameter of the house was at ground level; the other half consisted of a below-ground area measuring from two to five feet deep. The first floor contained a raised shelf about five or six feet wide, on which the men sat and slept. Below ground, the women and children cooked, ate, and slept.

The Yurok's deep feeling for the soil was reflected in the importance they gave to their dwelling sites, each of which had a name. Some sites were called *erkigeri* (a place where they prepared for dancing). Others were known as *ple'l* (meaning large), or *perkweri* (meaning behind the door). People referred to the name of a site rather than to the people who owned it

7

Yurok plank house.

or lived on it. A site name often designated the position of a house, the size or topography of the land on which it stood, or the ceremonial function performed in the dwelling. Yurok sweathouses also had names. The construction of a sweathouse was similar to that of a plank house. However, sweathouses were dug at least four feet over the entire extent. Men often used the sweathouses for meditation and sleeping.

Yurok tribes living in the mountains built cone-shaped dwellings. These were made by leaning together slabs of cedar bark or the bark of other conifers. The doorway of each house consisted of a bark slab which was used to close the entrance. Bedding was often made of Digger or of western white pine needles covered with the hides of deer, bear, or other animals.

The Japan Current is a stream of warm water in the Pacific which passes close to the northwest coast. The current creates water vapor which is blown onshore by prevailing winds. This produces a tropic-like climate. As the air and vapor condense and rise over the coastal mountains, they produce heavy rainfalls favorable to the growth of dense, coniferous forests.

There is no abrupt change in the physical environment between the coastal areas of California and the Northwest. The forests of the Northwest, however, contain mostly red and yellow cedars. Because Indians of the region found traveling by foot in these dense forests extremely difficult, they preferred to travel by water.

The ocean and rivers of the Pacific Northwest supplied the Indians with most of their food. They fished for salmon in the spring, and caught herring and trout throughout most of the year. They also gathered shellfish that abounded near the mouths of the rivers. In addition, several tribes built ocean-going canoes for deep-sea fishing and whale-hunting.

The Northwestern tribes were not only expert fishermen, they were also expert woodworkers. The cedar forests, which supplied them with their greatest source of natural materials, were used for almost every household need. Unlike the hardwood trees of the northeast which can break an axe, cedar can be split into straight, even pieces of timber. The wood is easily carved, and its bark was used to make clothing, baskets, nets, and a variety of other equipment.

Red and yellow cedars do not grow north of Admiralty Island in Alaska, just south of the capital city of Juneau. Thus, the Tlingit and other off-shore tribes had to trade furs and other commodities for the cedar with which they built their famous plank houses, totem poles, and ocean-going canoes. When necessary, they used hemlock for planking. Hemlock, however, is much harder to split and carve than cedar. The tallest cedars are found on the Queen Charlotte Islands, which stretch along the British Columbia coastline to Alaska.

The Kwakiutl of Johnston Strait, and a number of the Bella Coola tribes, lived along tidewater rivers on land that was often under water. They built large wooden dwellings on top of mounds of earth or shells into which they first sank huge poles. Platforms were then built around these poles. Some houses were erected on raised platforms as high as thiry feet off the ground. A long, notched tree was leaned from the dwelling platform to the ground, and served as stairs. Bella Coola tribes living further inland built dwellings with vertical planking and gabled roofs.

Kwakiutl dwelling.

Bellacoola dwelling and totem pole.

The Nootka, who were famous for their prosperous whaling industry, lived west of Canada's Vancouver Island. Their houses were built of horizontal cedar planking.

The Tsimshian, Tlingit, and Haida lived north of the Nootka, along the coast and on its adjacent islands, where suitable timber for building their dwellings was often scarce. A good tree had to be clear of branches for at least ten feet if it was to be used for posts. And the trunk had to be twice as long if it was to be used for ridgepoles. The tribes' usual method of felling a tree was to place hot rocks around the base until the fire ate through the wood. The charred wood was then slowly hacked away with a chisel-like tool. Wet seaweed or leaves were packed around the tree to keep the fire in check. It often took an entire day to fell one tree. The area where the tree fell was cleared and lined with logs that served to roll the tree into the water. When the tree was felled, its branches were cut off with stone axes. Many planks could be cut from one tree. Logs were split by driving wedges into the ends of the trees and pounding the wedge with a hammer stone until the log split in two. The planks were then tied to rafts and towed home where they were shaped with an axe or chisel.

The tribes' axes were made of jadeite, a mineral found only in one place near the Fraser River in Canada. Jadeite is not as hard as quartz, but it is a tough and serviceable stone. The axes were used to cut posts and to gouge out notches for the close fitting of the planks.

The totem poles of the Tlingit and their neighboring tribes represented pride in ancestry. The supernatural beings who decorated many of the poles symbolized original ancestors of the clan. Some clans placed their totem poles in front of their dwellings, while other tribes, such as the Haida, carved elaborate posts which were integral parts of their dwellings. Haida plank houses often had center posts which extended from the ground to above the roofs, and were carved in such a manner that the mouths of animals formed the doorways.

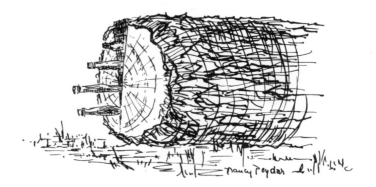

Wedges inserted in a log.

Wedges being pounded with a stone hammer.

Totem pole.

A great deal of time and labor were spent in the building of a wood plank house. A builder often enlisted the help of several families. Great feasts, ceremonies, and specific rituals accompanied all phases of construction. Sometimes an entire village became involved in building a house. The men did all the construction work, and the women prepared meals for the workers.

The framework of a plank house was often finished years

before the planking was prepared for the dwelling's walls. Planks were such valuable possessions that when home owners moved, they took their planks with them.

Plank house doorways were usually oval-shaped, raised several feet above the ground, and covered with elk skins. Most floors were covered with earth, but some were spread with sand or woven cattail mats. Very wealthy tribes even covered their floors with planks. Each family had its own fireplace, a hole dug in the floor and lined with heavy timbers or stones to keep the fire from spreading. There were no windows in a plank house, but this did not bother the dwellers who spent most of the winter before their fires.

DWELLING MATERIALS

Coast Live Oak

(Quercus agrifolia)

Coast live oak, sometimes called California live oak, is most often found in stands in the region between San Francisco and Baja California. The tree rarely grows more than fifty miles from the coast. Trees which grow in exposed areas near the ocean become shrubby. Live oak thrives in dry, gravelly soils, and will grow in altitudes ranging from sea level to 4,500 feet. Live oak is a low tree, with a short trunk that is divided close to the base into thick, crooked branches. Its dense, dark foliage remains on the tree for a year. The leaves, which are oval-shaped, and from one to four inches long, are edged with rigid teeth.

The inch-long, pointed acorn of the live oak was a staple food for many California Indians, who considered it superior to other kinds of acorns. The shell was removed, and the meat was soaked overnight in water to remove the tannin, an astringent with a bitter taste. The meats were then ground into flour either before or after they were roasted.

Live oak saplings were often used by the California Indians to build their brush-covered shelters. Where oak was not available, the California sycamore or white alder were used. If you are able to locate live oak saplings, you can build a small shelter and cover it with mats woven of tule.

Western Red Cedar

(Thuja plicata)

Western red cedar was preferred by the Indians of the Pacific Northwest for making their dugout canoes, totem poles, and

Coast live oak (*quercus agrifolia*).

plank houses. Red cedar often grows to a height of 200 feet; the best specimens are found near the coast.

The western red cedar is one of the largest trees of the Northwest coastal areas. It grows in company with the Douglas fir and the western hemlock. It can be found in latitudes ranging from sea level to 7,000 feet, but at higher elevations it often resembles a shrub.

Western red cedar is a cone-shaped tree with branches growing from the base up. When the tree is young, the branches

Western red cedar (*thuja plicata*).

reach upward; when it matures, the branches turn gracefully downward. The leaves have a lovely fragrance. Small and scale-like, they form lacy sprays, which are dark green on top with white triangular spots on their undersides. Each cone is a half-inch long. The cone seeds are double-winged, and they leave the cone during the autumn. The empty cone remains on the tree until the following summer.

The Indians stripped the bark from mature red cedars in twenty- to thirty-foot pieces. The bark was strong and durable and had a wide variety of uses, such as in weaving or making rope. Because the thinness of the bark offered the tree little protection when fire occurred, the tribes were extremely careful when felling one of the trees by their fire method. Fortunately, the moist environment of the cedar forests offered natural protection.

Today, we enjoy the qualities of red cedar just as the Indians did. The wood provides us with the bulk of our supply of house shingles and is an important lumber for use outdoors because it is usually impervious to decay and insects. In addition, glues, lacquers, paints, and varnishes easily adhere to the wood.

Tule or Bulrush
(Scirpus lacustris)

Tule, or bulrush, is a grass-like plant used by the Indians of California to weave mats and baskets.

There are over 150 species of bulrush in the world. The plant grows along the banks of ponds and streams, as well as in several feet of water.

Although the leaf of the bulrush is similar to grass, there are some distinct differences. Bulrush has a solid, triangular-shaped stem, while most grass stems are round and hollow. The lower part of a grass leaf has a sheath around the stem which is open on one side. The lower part of a bulrush stem has a closed sheath around the whole stem. Bulrush roots spread horizontal-

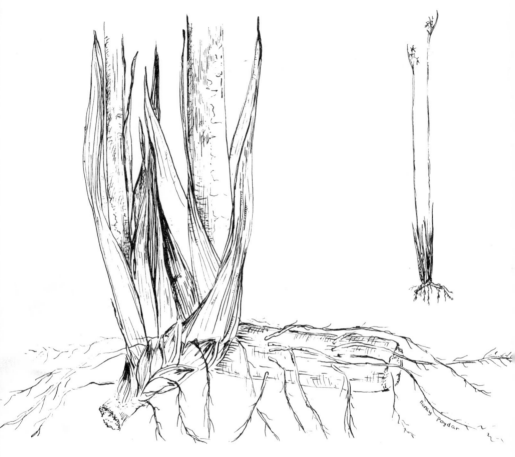

Tule, or bulrush (*scripus lacustris*).

ly underground. The strong, root portion of the bulrush was used by the Pomo Indians to make baskets. The long growth on the bud of the root was carefully cut or thinned so as not to damage the root system for the following year.

HOW TO BUILD A MINIATURE PLANK HOUSE

Materials

16	Cedar shingles, 7″ long (for house planking)
9	Cedar shingles, 18″ long (for roof planking)
8	6½″ posts, approximately 1″ in diameter*
4	2½″ posts, approximately ¾″ in diameter*
3	17″ ridgepoles, approximately ¾″ diameter*
4	11″ crossbeams, approximately ¾″ diameter*
8	7″ gable beams, approximately ¾″ diameter*
1	18″ x 24″ plywood piece for base
	Clay
	Household twine, or natural bark fibers, 2″ to 4″ wide and 3′ long
	Paper
	Putty knife
	Hammer
	Glue

*Young saplings or tree branches will not be the exact diameter.

A miniature plank house can be built with red cedar shingles. The shingles can be purchased from most lumber supply companies. Timber for framing a plank house can be gathered outdoors. Saplings or the branches of mature trees are suitable materials.

The wonderful qualities of cedar will become apparent as soon as you begin to work with red cedar shingles. The shingles can be easily split in a straight line by using a putty knife and a hammer. With care, the shingles can also be cut across the grain with the same tools.

1. Cut a 12" x 15" rectangle out of newspaper and lightly tack the pattern to a slightly larger plywood base.

2. Spread non-hardening modeling clay one-inch deep on the plywood outside the paper pattern. (The vertical planking will be set in the clay much like the Indians set their planks in the earth.)

3. Remove the paper pattern and glue eight 6½" posts onto the board along both sides (A).

4. Glue the four 11" crossbeams across the posts (B).

5. Glue two of the 17" ridgepoles onto the crossbeams along each side (C).

6. Glue the four 2½" posts to the center of the crossbeams (D).

7. Glue the third 17" ridgepole to the small 2½" posts (E).

8. Glue the eight 7" gable beams from the center top ridgepole to the outside ridgepoles (F).

9. After the timbers have been glued, tie them together with household twine or natural fibers made from tree bark. To tie the plank house timbers together with natural cordage, you will need a 3" length of basswood or cedar bark approximately 2" to 4" wide. Soak the bark in a jar of hot water to make it pliable. Strip away the outer bark, discard it, and use the strong inner fibers to tie the timbers together while the glue is drying.

10. It is not possible to gather saplings or tree branches that are exactly ¾" or 1" in diameter. Therefore, it is difficult to determine ahead of time the exact height of the finished plank house. The house should be completely framed before the cedar shingles are marked for cutting. To measure planks for the sides of the house, set the thick end of the 7" shingles on the plywood base and mark them at the top just

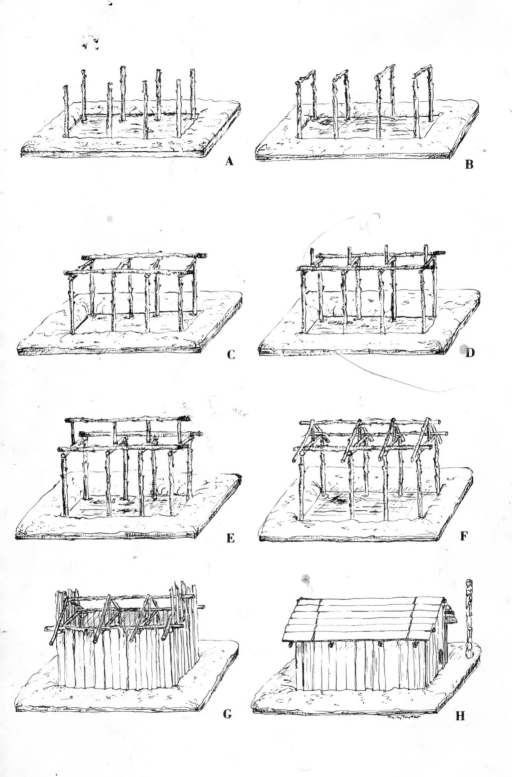

A

B

C

D

E

F

G

H

above the 11″ crossbeam (G). (To prevent the shingles from splitting unevenly, do not cut off this excess until the shingles are split into planks.)

11. To measure shingles for the front and back of the house, lean the thick end of the 7″ shingles against each end and mark them with a diagonal cut for the gable of the roof.

12. Cut the shingles into two-inch widths and cut off the excess length with a putty knife and a hammer.

13. Cut a small oval hole doorway in one of the planks.

14. Cut roof planks, about 2½″ wide, using the 18″ shingles. Tie each end of the planks with a long piece of twine. Starting at the outside edge, place the planks on the roof. Add additional planks, winding twine around each plank as it is placed on the roof. Planks should overlap.

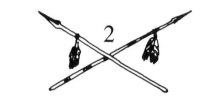

GREAT BASIN-PLATEAU

In distinct contrast to the adjacent Pacific coastal regions, the Great Basin-Plateau is a land of limited resources because coastal mountains rob the air of moisture. Wind brings moisture from the Pacific Ocean over the land. The moisture cools and becomes rain or snow upon the higher elevations of the area. Consequently, little moisture descends to the eastern slopes of the coastal ranges. This creates a desert in which cold is more prevalent than heat.

The Great Basin-Plateau extends from the Colorado River in the south to the great bend in the Fraser River in the north, and from the Rockies in the east to the Cascade and Sierra Mountains in the west. In the southern region, the Basin is a vast expanse of pebbly plains, flatlands encrusted with salt, and parched sands speckled with sagebrush and saltbush. It is also a land of brilliantly colored sandstone spires and awesome canyons. In the north, the high-plateau region consists of dense forests and snow-capped mountains.

Indians who lived in the Great Basin traveled constantly in search of food. Because fish and game were scarce, life was almost totally involved with survival; the threat of starvation was always present.

One of the Basin areas inhabited by the Indians was located on the western slopes of the Kaibab Plateau in southern Utah. There, springs in the sandstone cliffs created enough moisture for a variety of plant growth. At the base of the cliffs, the climate was almost arid. But just above the base, there were pinyon pines, juniper trees, and broad-leaved yuccas. At about 7,000 feet, the main timber were ponderosa pines, locusts, gambel oaks, blue spruce, balsams, and aspens. Squawbush, alders,

Kaibab permanent dwelling.

serviceberry, and oaks grew in the canyons, cattails and tules flourished near springs and streams.

The Kaibab tribes established permanent winter settlements along the springs at the base of the cliffs. They hunted in the higher elevations, and gathered plants and berries at all elevations. A typical Kaibab winter dwelling was made with the limb of a tree, which served as a ridgepole. Juniper poles were then leaned against the ridgepole to form a circle. The frame was covered with layers of juniper bark or with earth. Bark was laid on the floor, and green juniper branches were stacked across the entrance to keep out the cold. Although the dwellings did not have inside firepits, fires were usually kept burning just outside the doorways. Occupants kept warm by sleeping with their feet toward the fire. Household possessions were hung from the walls; bedding, when not in use, was rolled up and hung from a nearby tree. Both men and women worked on the dwelling construction. The men set up the framework of poles, and the women gathered bark and covered the framework. The habitats were temporary, lasting only one winter before the bark disintegrated.

The Kaibab also built a wall-less summer shelter by placing

Kaibab summer shelter.

25

willow branches across four tree limbs. When the tribe traveled to the higher elevations, they made temporary shelters by piling juniper branches in circles to heights of about four feet.

Other Great Basin tribes, such as the Paiute and the Ute lived in the territory ranging from southwestern Nevada to central Colorado. These tribes were less fortunate than the

Paiute brush shelter.

Kaibab because their available food sources were widely distributed, and they were forced to be on the move the year round.
Both the Ute and the Paiute lived in simple shelters made by
placing brush over frameworks of poles. The roofs of the shelters were almost entirely open.

Another region of the Great Basin is Death Valley, 140 miles

Ute shelter.

long and four to sixteen miles wide. The valley was formed by earth movements that caused the faulting and down-dropping of the area which lies between two ranges—the Panamint, Cottonwood, and Last Chance Mountains in the west, and the Grapevine and Funeral Mountains in the east.

The soils in the western part of the Valley, which is 282 feet below sea level, has a high salt and alkali content. A variety of saltbushes have adapted themselves to these conditions and can be found growing in sandy washes and on dunes. Above sea level, a dozen species of cacti may be found among the rocks and in well-drained soils. Several types of mesquite often form thickets, containing shallow ground water.

The Panamint tribe of Death Valley spent their winters in what is now called Furnace Creek; their summers were spent at nearby Shoshone and Beatty, where the temperatures are cooler. Their winter dwellings were dome-shaped, framed with willow or mesquite, and covered with desert brush or tule. The floors were excavated about a foot below ground level. The habitats contained indoor firepits and smoke holes in the roof.

The least favorable environments in any part of the Great

Panamint winter dwelling.

Basin were the Great Salt Lake Desert and Sevier Lake. Most of the rivers and creeks of the area are fed by rain and the melting snows of the Wasatch Mountains. The streams drain into both Great Salt and Sevier Lakes, neither of which has an outlet to the sea. Rainfall in the Great Salt Lake Desert is a mere five inches per year.

For the Gosuite Indians, who lived in the Great Salt Lake Desert, the year-round search for food extended over an area of 100 square miles. The easternmost boundary of the Gosuite territory included the Skull and Tooele Valleys. The Gosuite gathered most of the stone and wood for their household possessions and shelters in the mountains east of these two valleys. Many groups of the tribe lived in natural rock caves. Other groups built conical structures of juniper poles covered with bark and branches. A typical shelter was a three-foot-high circular enclosure constructed of stacked sagebrush and branches of cedar. They were very flimsy shelters that did little more than protect the Indians from the wind.

Food resources were more plentiful in the Plateau region north of the Basin. Fish abounded in the rivers and streams; berries, nuts, and camass plants and other flora grew in the Bitterroot Mountains; and deer flourished in mountain pastures. The camass plant, a member of the lily family, was the primary food source of the Plateau Indians. Each summer the bulbs of the plant were roasted and dried for winter storage. This crop was as important to the Plateau tribes as corn was to the farming tribes in the southwest and elsewhere. The Plateau Indians were able to store enough camass roots to allow them to remain in their winter villages along the rivers and streams of the narrow canyons that protected them from the drifting snows of the high plateau. It was still necessary, however, for the men to continue to hunt all winter.

One of the most powerful of the Plateau tribes was Nez Percé. The tribes traveled extensively, and each spring they moved to their favorite fishing, hunting, and root-digging grounds. Villages that shared areas, or held land in common, granted families exclusive rights to preferred spots. This happened most often with favorite fishing areas.

Salmon were caught in September and October and again at high-water time in spring. Most of the catch was stored for winter use.

Hunting was easiest in the fall, when deer migrated to the lower canyons. Deerskin was used by most of the clans, but elk was preferred for making moccasins, dresses, and other clothing. Antelope, however, was prized for its water-repellent qualities and its pliability when wet.

Many clans of the Nez Percé wintered in the valleys of the Snake, Clearwater, and Salmon Rivers and summered in the Bitterroot Mountains to the west. Other clans wintered along the Imaha, Joseph, and Snake Rivers and summered in the uplands of the Wallowa Basin—an excellent grazing spot for deer.

The Nez Percé built inverted V-shaped dwellings that held several families. The frame was formed by leaning together two sets of forked timbers. A ridgepole was then placed between the timbers, and additional poles were leaned against the ridgepole. The entire structure was covered with mats. Ponderosa, also

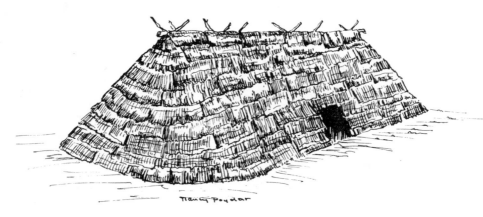

Nez Percé dwelling.

Thompson Indians covering a tipi with tule mats.

called western yellow pine, was the tribe's favorite framing timber. Floors were dug at least two feet below the ground, and the excavated earth was piled against the outside edge of the dwellings. Summer shelters were necessary when the Nez Percé traveled in the mountains and on the prairies. The shelters were made of mats removed from the winter dwellings.

In the early 1700s, when the Nez Percé acquired horses, they quickly adopted the habits' of their neighbors on the Plains. Each year, groups crossed the Rocky Mountains as soon as the snow had melted in the passes to hunt buffalo. They also used the tipi of the Plains Indians, but the Nez Percé covered theirs with tule mats.

The Thompson Indians of British Columbia and the Umatilla Indians of Oregon also imitated their neighbors on the Plains. They, too, built tipis and covered them with tule mats. The mats were tied on to the tipi, starting at the bottom and working up. Matting was held down by placing additional poles on top.

Still another dwelling used by the Indians of the Plateau was a semi-subterranean one. These dwellings were dug deep in the ground, and were either oval or elliptical in shape. The sides were lined with slabs of bark or timbers. Four posts were set in the ground in the center of the dugout area, and crossbeams were placed across the posts to form a square. Additional posts were then leaned from the square to the slabs of bark or timbers

Semi-subterranean dwelling.

33

FACING PAGE: Umatilla tipi.

which lined the pit. More poles covered the roof, which was thatched with grass and completely covered with earth. The entrance was the smoke hole in the top. Some of these houses were quite large and could accommodate several families.

DWELLING MATERIALS

Sierra Juniper or Western Juniper

(Juniperus occidentalis)

Sierra junipers grow in areas where few trees can exist. Under good conditions, they may reach a height of 60 feet, but they often grow no higher than a shrub. Sierra junipers can be found

Sierra juniper or western juniper (*juniperus occidentalis*).

in exposed areas, and on dry, gravelly slopes in Oregon, western Nevada, in the mountain regions of southeastern Washington and western Idaho, and along the eastern and southern foothills of the Sierra Nevadas. They are also found throughout the Great Basin area.

A Sierra juniper has a broad crown and a short, fat trunk. The trunk is forked at the base or in the middle, and these lower branches extend horizontally. The roots are close to the surface, which enables the tree to take advantage of meager water supplies. The roots take hold in rock crevices and spread into the surrounding rocky soil. A Sierra juniper is able to withstand strong winds.

Sierra junipers have two kinds of foliage: needle-like leaves and scale-like leaves, which overlap each other in groups of three. The latter type of leaves clasp the twigs and form rounded stems. They are pale green, with small glandule pits on their backs. This thick foliage was extremely useful to the Indians of the Great Basin who used it to make primitive shelters.

Juniper berries are bluish-black, about one-fourth to one-third of an inch long. They have two or three pits, surrounded by dry flesh. The juniper does not have a true berry, but a modified cone with connected scales that are fleshy.

Juniper bark is a cinnamon color. It is strong, stringy, about one-half inch thick, and divided into wide furrows. Juniper wood is aromatic, soft, but durable.

Ponderosa Pine

(Pinus ponderosa)

Ponderosa pine, also called western yellow pine, grows on mountain slopes, in dry valleys, and on high mesas. It is common in Washington, Oregon, western Montana, northern Idaho, on the slopes of the Sierra Nevadas, and on the California coast. It also grows on lava beds, on sun-baked mesas, and on plains where other trees cannot survive.

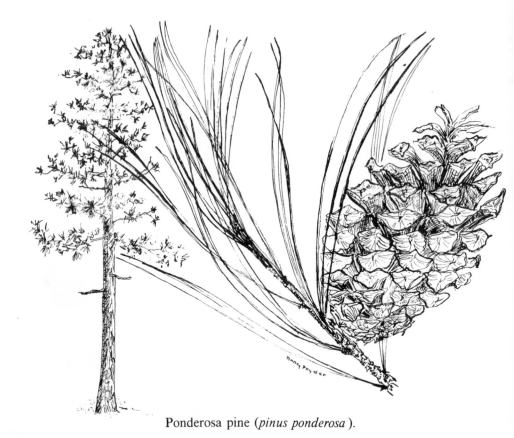

Ponderosa pine (*pinus ponderosa*).

Ponderosa pines reach heights of 230 feet and grow as large as eight feet in diameter. Their leaves, or needles, grow in clusters of two or three. Each leaf is from five to ten inches long, and remains on a twig for three to seven years.

Clusters of the tree's brown cones grow to six inches in length. Young cones are bright green or purple; when they mature, they become a reddish-brown. The scales of the cones spread open for the seeds to escape.

Ponderosa pine is relatively light in weight, strong, and fine-grained. Unfortunately, it is subject to a number of insects and fungi. Disease control is difficult because the trees are usually scattered over a broad area and are often inaccessible. Their bark is scaly and paper-like. In older trees it is nearly black. When food sources were scarce, the Indians stripped bark off the ponderosa pine early in spring and ate the mucilaginous layer of forming wood. The branches, when cut, have an aroma of orange peel.

HOW TO BUILD A PAIUTE WIKIUP

Materials

15 to 20   7' branch poles (1" in diameter)
              Boughs and brush (for cover)
              Pointed stick
              Pruning scissors
              Hand trowel (optional)

The wikiup was probably the simplest shelter ever constructed by the Indians of North America. It was the only kind used by the Paiute Indians of the Great Basin, and it was used as a temporary dwelling by the Menomini tribes of the Great Lakes region.

A Paiute wikiup was generally in the form of a semi-circle, with poles stuck in the ground around two-thirds of the circle. Wikiups were also often built of sticks and dead tree limbs, and covered with leaves, brush, and a variety of other materials in the area.

1.   Draw a circle on the ground with a pointed stick to outline the wikiup (A).
2.   For the frame, locate 15 to 20 branches, each about 7' high and 1" in diameter. You may use saplings or the branches of older trees.
3.   Before you place the branch poles in the ground, deter-

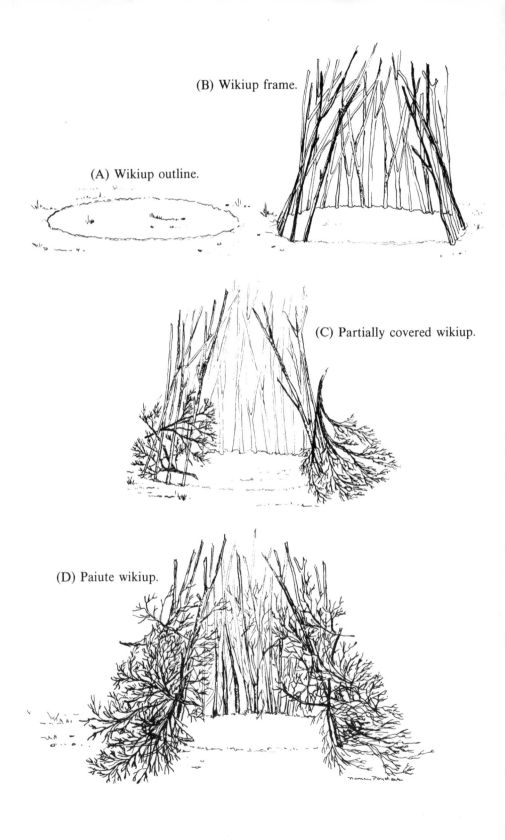

(B) Wikiup frame.

(A) Wikiup outline.

(C) Partially covered wikiup.

(D) Paiute wikiup.

mine the direction of the prevailing winds. The wikiup should have its covered side to the wind. Push the poles into the ground around the edge of the circle and lean them toward the center (B). It is helpful to have forks on some of the poles so they will support each other when they are leaned together. Place the poles as close together as possible; otherwise the covering materials will fall through the openings.

4. Gather enough boughs from a Sierra juniper tree (see page 34) to cover the frame. You will have to place the boughs carefully so that they will stay on the frame without slipping off. Weave the tips of the boughs together, or weave them between the framing poles. Use any method you can think of to keep the covering in place without tying it on (C). Sierra juniper may be used in combination with other pines of the desert. You may also use a variety of brush for covering. Remember, however, that it takes a long time for plants to grow in the desert. They should never be pulled up by the roots. It is always wise to prune from mature trees and shrubs.

SOUTHWEST

The first inhabitants of the Southwest used the sandstones of the mesas, clay, and timber from the mountain forests to build their homes and shelters. The arid environment of the region has helped to preserve many Southwestern Indian dwellings and artifacts.

The word, desert, often conjures up visions of shifting sand dunes and cactus plants—a land without rain, water, or life. Yet only a tiny part of the Southwest fits that description. For the most part, the area is an arid expanse of treeless valley floors, strewn with mesas, buttes, and sandstone formations. In the canyons there are streams, where willow trees, cattails, and rushes flourish. There are also snow-capped mountains within view, where pinyon pine, spruce, fir, and aspen grow. The plants that grow on the valley floors have adapted themselves to life with a limited amount of water. The plants have very small leaves, and they grow far apart.

At first, the early inhabitants of the area lived in the natural caves in the canyon walls. The tribes originally gathered seeds, berries, and the roots of plants, and hunted small desert animals. Eventually, they planted crops and became farmers.

Desert sandstone was widely used by these early inhabitants. Many of the mesas in their area are made of porous sandstone that readily holds water. Below the layers of sandstone, there is a layer of shale, which is not porous and will not allow water to pass through. Thus, when heavy rains occur, water is held in a mesa's upper layers of sandstone until it seeps through to the layer of shale. It then travels along the shale and emerges

at the base of a cliff. The Pueblo Indians planted their corn, beans, and squash near these emerging springs. To insure a successful harvest, they developed elaborate irrigation systems.

The tribes were able to feed hundreds and sometimes thousands of people in one location. By the sixteenth century, they left the canyon caves and lived in multi-storied, flat-topped dwellings which clung to the sides of the canyons. Spanish explorers called these dwellings *pueblos,* the Spanish word for villages.

The Pueblo had little wood to build their homes, but they had stone and clay with which they made adobe bricks. Some of their dwellings were built of sandstone that blended so well with the canyon walls that only a very experienced eye could see them. Eventually, the tribe moved to the top of the mesas, where they built apartment-type dwellings.

The Pueblo were divided into clans; each clan lived in areas divided by terraces. The terraces served several purposes. In addition to being passageways from one home to another, they were used as communal kitchens. Tribal members entered their windowless dwellings by ladders in holes of the roofs. Ladders also led from one terrace to another and could be pulled up in case of attack.

Another tribe of the region, the Hopi, sited their homes for maximum exposure to the morning sun and for protection from cold winds. The Hopi and other desert Indians made durable, sun-dried bricks with clay and water. The bricks were usually made on the banks of nearby streams. To make the bricks, a fire of sagebrush and sedge grass was started. When the fire was partly live coals and partly ashes, the clay was thrown onto the fire. When the clay was cooled enough to handle, it was shaped into bricks.

Another desert-dwelling tribe, the Apache, built small, skin-covered tipis, with frames made of saplings. The tipis were easily erected, and could be folded and moved in a matter of minutes.

43

FACING PAGE: Pueblo dwelling.

Pueblo of San Felipe, New Mexico.

The Navajo Indians, who migrated to the desert from Central America, stayed and mingled with the Pueblo who taught them to farm and to weave. By the 1800s, the Navajo were well established in Arizona, where they built dome-shaped or conical earth-and-timber dwellings, called *hogans.* Hogans were generally located in box canyons or at the base of cliffs. They had to be far enough away from a spring so that animals would not be frightened away when they came to water. Like all Indian habitats, the hogan was so unobtrusive it could not be easily spotted on the desert floor.

To build a hogan, the Navajo made a trip to the mountains to fell pinyon pines for the frame. Three trees, forked about six or eight feet above the ground, were burned at the base until they fell. They were then stripped of branches and bark to make them lighter to carry. Two straight, but smaller, timbers were also obtained for the hogan's doorway. The doorway faced east because tribal members did not want anything to come between them and the rising sun when they went outside to pray each morning. Also, prevailing winds were from the west, and these often were very cold in winter.

When the Navajo began the construction of their hogans, the forked ends of the timbers were braced together at the top by interlocking forks. The two timbers for the doorway were then placed against the forked timbers. Limbs of pinyon pine and cedar, plus a variety of twigs, were laid against the timbers and secured with yucca. The entire structure was then covered with cedar bark. Finally, six inches of earth were added for insulation and waterproofing.

Before moving in, a Navajo family performed a ceremony. If a person died in the hogan, it was sealed off. If there was a window in the hogan, the deceased was pulled out through the window before the dwelling was sealed. Then the hogan was burned or abandoned.

There were traditional places in a hogan for each member of the family. After entering, the women turned right toward the

Hogan frame.

Navajo sweathouse.

kitchen. The men turned left. Only the head of the family was allowed to occupy the rear of the hogan, the place of honor. Thus, even though a hogan allowed very little privacy, traditional use of the interior created distinct interior areas.

Another type of hogan was made by excavating the side of a hill. The exposed portion was sometimes built of stone or wood. Sweathouses, though somewhat smaller than the hogans, were often built in this way.

The Navajo also built several kinds of summer shelters. The most popular style was made by imbedding four forked timbers in the ground. Crossbeams extended from fork to fork. Sage and desert brush were laid across the timbers to form a flat roof which kept out the hot summer sun. Another kind of summer shelter was made by stripping the branches from a tree. The branches were then piled four or five feet high in a semi-circle and covered with hides or blankets. When fresh pinyon pine branches were used for these shelters, they had to be sealed with mud to prevent the resin from dripping. Still another type of

Navajo summer shelter.

summer shelter was made by placing two forked timbers in the ground, extending a beam across them and leaning cedar boughs against the beam to form an inverted V.

South of the Gila River in southern Arizona live the Pima and Papago Indians, whose ancestors were probably the Hoho-kams. The giant saguaro cactus grows in this region. A mature plant is taller than a man, and as thick as a pine tree trunk. The saguaro has ridges of white thorns instead of leaves. Its fruit is still harvested each year by modern-day Indians. The saguaro does not decay when it dies, but dries up, yielding interior wood which is hard and durable. Wood from dead saguaro plants was used to frame Pima and Papago dwellings and to make tools.

The Pima and Papago were outstanding basketmakers, and they built dome-shaped dwellings which resembled their baskets. Because there is so little rainfall in this area, their dwellings did not have to be waterproofed or heavily insulated. A home was made with a framework of four forked timbers, with straight timbers laid across (fork-to-fork) to form a square. Stems from the ocotillo bush were leaned against the cross-beams and tied at the top with bear grass which often grows from 10 to 15 feet long.

Ocotilla bush on right; mule cactus on left.

DWELLING MATERIALS

Pinyon Pine

(Pinus edulis)

The Navajo had to travel to the dry foothills, slopes, and canyons of the Rocky Mountains for timber for the framework of their hogans. They used pinyon pine, which grows at elevations between 5,000 and 8,000 feet.

Pinyon pine does well in any kind of sandy, gravelly soil, and

Pinyon pine (*pinus edulis*).

it roots in the lava-like soils common to the Southwest. Because it can withstand both drought and freezing, it also survives on exposed slopes.

Pinyon pine usually grows up to 20 feet high, and its branches spring from the trunk six or eight feet from the ground. These natural forks were used to good advantage by the Indians of the Southwest when building their dwellings. The tree was cut above the fork so that the forks would interlock when leaned together to form the framework of a hogan.

There are four pines in the Southwest which bear edible nuts. Pinyon, or *pinus edulis,* was preferred by the Indians because of its large, tasty nuts. To identify a *pinus edulis,* look for needles that appear in clusters of two (occasionally you will find three). The needles are sharply pointed, curved, and from one to two inches long. Young trees have bright, bluish-green needles. The cones, which are egg-shaped, shiny, and yellow-brown, mature during the second season. The nut-like seeds are contained in the middle of the cone. The tribes roasted the nuts as soon after picking as possible. They were then made into flour.

You may also identify pinyon pine by its distinctive, reddish-brown bark, which is formed in ridges.

Rocky Mountain Juniper

(Juniperus scopulorum)

Rocky Mountain juniper, sometimes called Rocky Mountain red cedar, was used by the Navajo for their hogans. Juniper twigs were set down against the pinyon pine timbers of the frame and then covered with earth.

Junipers can be found from Alberta, Canada, to New Mexico, and from British Columbia to eastern Oregon, Nevada, and northern Arizona. The trees grow best in canyons where the ground is rich and moist. They are most often found, however, on dry ridges and on mountain slopes. When growing in the

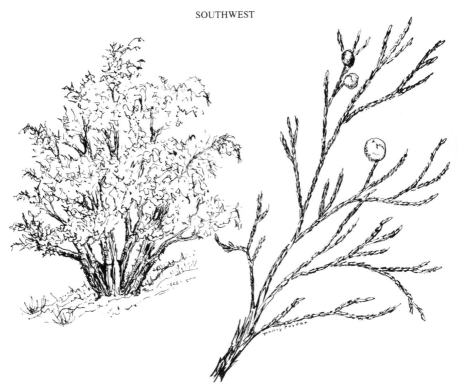

Rocky Mountain juniper (*juniperus scopulorum*).

open, a juniper becomes a shrubby tree about 15 to 20 feet tall. The trunk is divided near the ground into many thick branches.

Twigs of the juniper are four-sided when young, but become rounded within three or four years. The green leaves are small and often tapered at the ends.

The fruit of the juniper ripens at the end of the second season, when it becomes spherical and measures about one-third of an inch in diameter. Clear blue in color, the fruit contains a pulp and has one or two shiny brown seeds.

You can identify the juniper by its dark reddish-brown or gray bark, which is divided into flat ridges.

The wood of Rocky Mountain juniper is durable, and would be an important lumber source except for its small size and scattered growth.

HOW TO BUILD A NAVAJO SUMMER SHELTER

Materials

2   6' timbers (3″ in diameter)
4   6' timbers (4″ in diameter, forked at one end)
Pinyon pine, juniper, a variety of bark and brush
Hand trowel or shovel

Navajo summer shelters protected the tribe from the hot summer sun. One of the summer shelters still used on Navajo reservations in Arizona is made with four forked pinyon pine timbers, which support a roof of brush, bark, and juniper boughs. To make a five-foot-square shelter, it is necessary to mark off four corners. This can be done without measuring tools, using the timbers collected for framing the shelter.

1. Obtain two fairly straight young pinyon pine trunks, each approximately 6' long and 3″ in diameter. You will also need four young pinyon trunks, each 6' long and approximately 4″ in diameter, forked at one end.
2. Place one of the straight timbers (unforked) on the ground and dig two holes in the ground six inches in from each end. Because the forked timbers that go in these holes are fairly large, the holes should be dug at least eight inches deep (A).
3. Place two of the forked timbers in the holes that have been dug, making sure the forks face each other (B).
4. Take the straight timber used to measure, and place it between the two forked timbers (C).
5. The second set of forked timbers should be parallel to the first set and about five feet away. To mark the second two corners of the square, place the straight

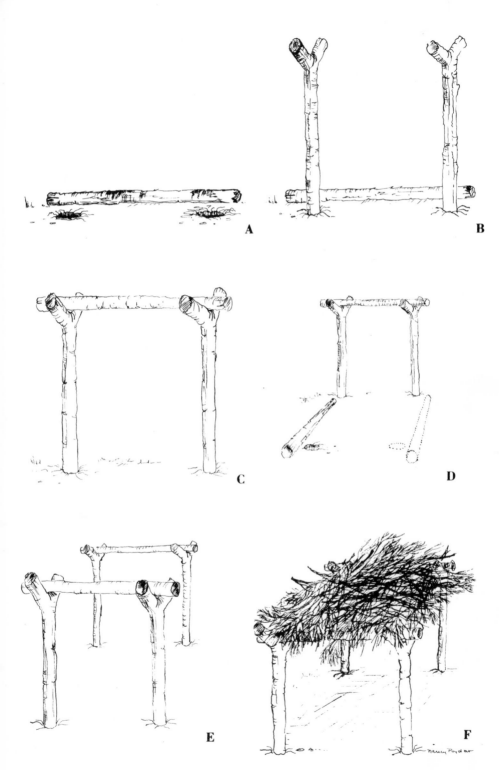

How to build a Navajo summer shelter.

timber on the ground, using it to measure the distance from the first one and then the other of the two forked timbers already in the ground. Because the square is to be five feet and the straight timber used to measure is six feet, you will want to dig the hole approximately one foot in from the end of the measuring timber (D).

6. Place the second set of forked timbers in the holes you have just dug. Again, be sure the forks are facing each other.

7. Place the remaining straight timber between the second set of forked timbers. You now have a frame for a five-foot-square shelter (E).

8. Collect limbs of pinyon pine, juniper, plus a variety of bark or brush, and place them across the roofing frame. Six- to seven-foot lengths of juniper placed across the two roof timbers will provide good support for lighter-weight brush and bark. Continue to add to the roof until all the spaces are filled and sun cannot get through (F).

THE PLAINS

The popular image of the Native American reflects the tribes of the Plains. When we think of a North American Indian, we sometimes picture a tall brave on a horse in front of a painted tipi. Few Indian dwellings have received as much attention as the Plains tipi. The skin-covered dwelling was so well suited for prairie life that the U.S. Army used it as a model for the Army's portable canvas tent.

The grasslands of the Plains extend from central Canada to Texas, and from Indiana to the Rockies. It is easy to see why early explorers always referred to the Plains as "a sea of grass." There are short-grass prairies and tall-grass prairies. The tall grasses grow on the eastern edge of the Plains; short grass is found on the western edge. In eastern Kansas, there are both short and tall grasses. The tall grasses once grew as high as 12 feet. The short-grass prairie results from strong winds which blow over the Rockies and from scant precipitation in the area.

Today, much of the grassland is gone. With the help of modern irrigation systems, large farming areas of the Plains produce high yields of corn, wheat, and grazing lands for cattle.

The Blackfoot, Crow, and Comanche were among the tribes that lived in the Central Plains. They hunted the buffalo for its meat; hide (for clothing); and horns, sinew, and bones (for tools and utensils).

Tribes living along the borders of the open prairie often resembled their neighbors to the east, west, and south with whom they shared a more common environment. These fringe tribes combined buffalo hunting with farming, fishing, and the gathering of berries, nuts, and various plants.

Tribes in the Central Plains moved with the roaming herds of buffalo, and often traveled up to 400 miles during each season. When cold weather approached, buffalo that had summered in Nebraska, the Dakotas, and Wyoming headed south to winter in Texas and New Mexico. Herds which had spent the summer in Montana migrated to Wyoming and Colorado; and herds that had summered in Saskatchewan, Canada, moved south to Montana in winter.

Two nomadic tribes of the northern Plains were the Crow and the Blackfoot. They, too, left the open spaces in fall and established winter camps in the valleys. The tribes built some of the largest tipis of all the Plains Indians. These well-proportioned dwellings were covered with beautifully whitened skins. Like most Indian homes, they were warm and durable.

The Blackfoot extended their tipi poles four to six feet above the top of the cover. The Crow had much less of an extension, and their tipis were comparatively stubby in appearance. The tipis of both tribes were erected in grassy areas among the trees of river valleys, where the horses could graze until snowfall. In winter, when most of the grazing land was covered, horses often ate the bark of cottonwood trees.

Sundance scene in tipi village.

Tipi villages were most often clustered in a circle around an open space where ceremonial dances were held. The most prominent families lived in painted tipis on the inside perimeter of the circle.

A typical tipi was the Arapaho lodge, made of skins sewn together with buckskin thongs.

Long before a tipi was erected, the women started making sinew for thread. Sinew, or animal tendon, was used by many tribes for sewing hides together because of its great strength. Indian women also made needles and awls out of buffalo bone. When the men brought in fresh hides, the woman tanned and stretched them.

The women also gathered tipi poles from mountain slopes and river valleys. Pine was chosen for its great height and straightness. The trees were stripped of bark and twigs and trimmed until very smooth because a bump on a tipi pole could

Arapaho buffalo-skin tipi.

cause a hole in the tipi's covering. The poles were then dried
in the sun to make them lighter and easier to handle.

When a woman was ready to make the covering, she prepared a great quantity of food. Then she invited her friends to
eat with her. If they accepted, it meant they were willing to help
with the work. To sew together and decorate the hides of an
average dwelling took a group of women almost an entire day.

The woman also chose the tipi site. She made sure the ground
was level, that there were no animal holes in the ground, and
that the spot was well drained. Before the tipi was put up, the
head of the family set up a tripod on which he hung his medi-
cine bundles to show his reverence for the sun.

Tipi construction began by placing four poles on the ground.
Some tribes preferred a three-pole frame, which created a spi-
ral-like appearance. Four-pole tipis made the tipi's base very
wide in proportion to its height. The poles were lashed together
while on the ground, about four feet from the top. They were

then raised and spread out at the base. Additional poles were leaned against the topmost fork, formed by the first four poles. The more poles used, the tighter the skin could be stretched around the tipi. The cover, a semicircle of skins, was placed on the ground and tied at the middle to a long pole. The pole and the cover were then lifted and placed at the back of the tipi frame. The two ends of the cover were wrapped around the frame and secured with wooden pegs in the front. The entrance consisted of a dressed skin of buffalo calf or a coyote pelt. The door faced south because prevailing winds were from the north. Two "ear" pieces were added last. These looked like elephant ears or a pair of wings, and could be moved to regulate the draft around the smoke hole. A firepit, outlined with stone, was located in the center of the tipi, and a tripod was placed over the hearth to hold the cooking utensils and food.

The Blackfoot tribes lined the lower inside rim of their tipis with beautifully tanned and decorated hides. These hangings served to insulate the tipi in both summer and winter by creating an air pocket between the inside and outside skins. The bottom edges of the tipi could also be pulled up in summer to allow the breeze to come in; grass and sod were often stacked along the outside edges in winter to keep out cold winds. The tipi floor was lined with grass and covered with skins with the hair sides uppermost. When the tipi was finished, and before the occupants moved in, a sagebrush fire was lit inside the dwelling to preserve the skins by smoking them.

When the tribe broke camp, the women dismantled the tipis and loaded up the horses that were tied to a *travois,* a wheel-less cart that was dragged by the horses. Tipi covers were carried on the backs of the animals.

The tipi covers, if well cared for, lasted for several years, even though the sinew used to sew the hides often broke. Some tipis were colorfully decorated with birds, animals, stars, and other symbolic art. Red and brown paints were made from berries, nuts, clay, and river muds; black was made from charcoal;

Travois.

Crow woman decorating skins.

Pawnee village.

green from the algae of stagnant waters; and yellow from bile which collects in buffalo gallstones. The skins were painted before they were taken off their stretchers.

The Arikara, Omaha, Mandan, Pawnee, and lower Missouri River tribes were primarily farmers. They built earth-covered lodges and lived in permanent villages.

The northern waters of the Missouri River cut a deep channel through walls of flat-topped clay and tableland. On bluffs above the river, and in the open prairie below it, lived the Mandan Indians. They were very successful farmers, who were often raided by other tribes for their stored crops. For protection, the Mandan fortified their villages with palisades, made by placing eighteen-foot timbers in the ground. Their dwellings were earth lodges, built closely together. Mandan villages had a space in their centers, where festivals and ceremonies were held and games were played. Their lodges were 40 to 60 feet in diameter, and excavated a foot or so below ground. They were dome-shaped, with framework constructions similar to those used in the grass houses of the southeast. Four to eight large, forked posts were set in the ground to support the heavy crossbeams that formed the roof. Willow branches were laid around the outside, and a heavy thatch of coarse grass was arranged over the branches. A thick coat of sod, cut and applied like shingles, was placed over the grass. The floor was prepared by tamping the earth and flooding it with water. Dried grass was then spread over the earth and set on fire. This was tamped down again, more grass was added, and another fire was set. The process was repeated until the floor was hard and level. These types of floors were very easy to keep clean.

In the center of each floor was a stone-edged firepit with a smoke hole above it. Beds were made of round poles lashed together with thongs. Buffalo hides were stretched across the frame, and also served as blankets and pillows. To provide privacy, each bed was screened off with a beautifully decorated hide that was hung from the frame of the dwelling.

DWELLING MATERIALS

Lodgepole Pine

(Pinus contorta)

Lodgepole pine may be found from the Alaskan coast to Mendocino County in California, where it grows in bogs and swamps, near sand dunes, and around the margins of tide pools. The tree changes its appearance and habits when it grows inland, especially near the Rocky Mountains. It is the prevailing tree on the Yellowstone Plateau in northwestern Wyoming and on the slopes of the Rocky Mountains, where it grows at elevations of 10,000 to 12,000 feet. It may also be found as far south as southern Colorado and as far north as the Bitterroot Mountains along the Idaho-Montana border. In the Rockies, lodge-

Lodgepole pine (*pinus contorta*).

pole pines grow quite tall and have slender trunks. These trees were valued for tipi frames by the Indians of the Plains.

The topmost branches of lodgepole pines form a pyramid. The leaves are yellow-green, and they vary from one to three inches in length. The cones are oval-shaped, from ¾ " to 2" long, and their scales have prickles on them. The seeds of the lodgepole germinate quickly after a forest fire because heat opens the cones and allows the seeds to escape. Lodgepole pines often re-seed themselves after a forest fire. In some areas of the west, these trees have replaced spruce, fir, and other pines.

HOW TO BUILD A TIPI

Materials

> 10 to 12   8′ poles
> 18 to 20   Wooden pegs
>   3   Twin-sized bedsheets
>   Canvas or felt pieces
>   Ball of twine
>   Scissors
>   Pencil
>   Ruler
>   Binding (optional)
>   Sewing machine, or large-eye needle and heavy duty thread
>   Fabric paint or waterproof felt-tipped markers (assorted colors)

The word *tipi* comes from the Siouan root *ti,* which means to dwell.

There are a number of different kinds of tipis, all of which have the same conical shape. Tipis were generally used by nomadic people who needed a fairly simple shelter which was easy to put up and take down. Many of the larger tipis took a great amount of skill and hard work to build. Tipi construction was part of a woman's chores.

A tipi of your own can be used all year round.

1. Locate ten to twelve poles, each at least 8′ long. You can cut branches from large trees that need pruning, or you may want to buy bamboo or cedar poles, such as the kind used for staking plants.

2. Sew together three twin-sized bedsheets. Along one of the sides (A) turn under a wide hem about 6″ deep.

How to build a tipi.

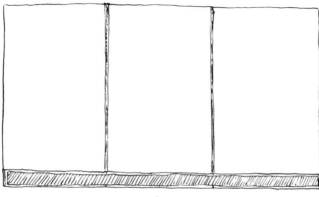

A

Marking the center of a tipi cover.

Sew a piece of canvas or felt to it. This will allow you to cut holes along the edge for the wooden pegs. (A strong backing that does not fray will not require bound buttonholes.)

3. Mark a dot in the middle of the three sheets on the hemmed side.

4. Cut a piece of twine 7' long and tie it to the end of a pencil. Hold the end of the twine on the dot in the middle of the hemmed edge. Have a friend draw a half-circle with the pencil (B). (Remember to mark and cut with the seamed side up.)

5. Along the hemmed edge in the center of the sheets, mark a spot for the smoke hole. Hold a 5" length of twine attached to a pencil on the mark and draw a small half-circle (C).

6. Along the same hemmed edge, measure 18" in from each end and mark a spot for the door holes. Hold an 8" length of twine attached to a pencil on the marks and draw half-circles (C).

7. Between the smoke hole and the door holes, mark where the pegs will be inserted (D). You will need eight to ten pegs between the smoke hole and doorway and two to three pegs from the doorway to the ground.

8. Cut out the tipi cover according to the lines you have drawn. (It is a good idea to bind the edges of both the smoke hole and door holes with a strong binding before the cover is put on.)

9. Lash three or four poles together as illustrated in (E).

10. Stand the poles on end and spread them out at the base.

11. Lean additional poles against the first three or four poles. The more poles used, the tighter the cover will fit.

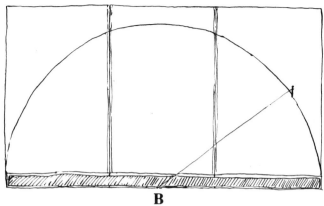

B

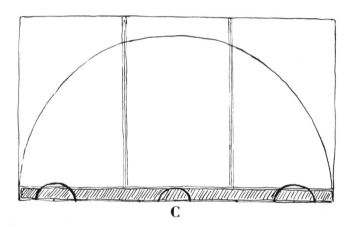

C

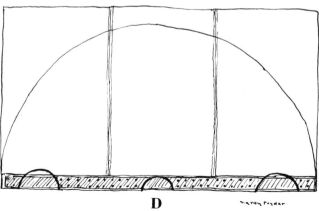

D

Nancy Pryder

Cutting out a tipi cover.

12. Put the cover around the tipi and pin it together down the front, matching the cut-outs.
13. Add wooden pegs when everything is adjusted. Pegs may be cut from a branch.

If you want to paint your tipi, do so after the sheets are cut out. Lay the tipi cover on a large, flat surface and draw designs

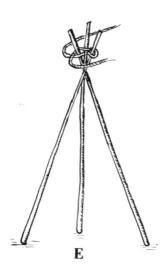

E

Four-pole tipi frame.

on the base. Color with commercial paint designed for use on fabric.

To keep the wind out of the tipi in winter, pack earth around its bottom edge. In summer, pull up the edges and allow the breeze to blow through.

Tipi frame with added poles.

5

SOUTHEAST

The territory occupied by Indian tribes living in the southeastern portion of the United States extended from the Appalachian Mountains in Virginia and Tennessee, westward into Arkansas, southward along the Atlantic coast to the tip of Florida, and along the Gulf of Mexico from Florida to Texas. The Creek Indians lived in Georgia and Alabama, the Choctaw and Chickasaw tribes were located in Mississippi and Louisiana, the Caddo Indians in Louisiana and Texas, and Timucua on Cumberland Island as well as the adjacent Georgia mainland and northern Florida. The Cherokee lived in the Appalachian Mountains and in northern Georgia, and the Catawba and Tuscarora tribes dwelled in the western regions of the Carolinas.

The Appalachian Mountains dominate the eastern portion of the United States, just as the Rockies dominate the west. The Appalachians range from Newfoundland in the north to the Great Smokies in the south. From the mountains eastward stretch the coastal plains that contain rich deposits of limestone because the entire area was once a sea bottom.

Limestone is a soft rock, formed from deposits of once-living organisms such as shell, coral, and algae. It is responsible for the rich farmland of the Shenandoah Valley and for the famous bluegrass in Kentucky. West of the Appalachians are valleys and ridges that eventually give way to grassland.

The Indians farmed the coastal plains along the Gulf and eastern seaboards. In Virginia and the Carolinas, they cultivated bountiful crops of corn and tobacco. Along the immediate coast, fish and shellfish were so plentiful that only small gardens were planted.

The Caddo Indians of Texas and Louisiana lived in large, grass lodges that looked like giant haystacks. These dwellings were difficult to build. Whole trees were set in the ground close together and laced with willow branches. This framework was

Caddo camp; framework of summer hut in foreground.

Choctaw palmetto dwelling.

then heavily thatched with grass. Additional bundles of grass were placed atop each dwelling to give it a decorated appearance. Most homes had sleeping lofts. Bed frames, usually covered with reed mats, were raised off the floor. Mattresses were often made of deer skins stuffed with Spanish moss or shredded corn husks. Floors were covered with closely woven mats, decorated with pictures of birds, animals and flowers. Once the dwelling was finished, the owners prepared a feast for all of the workers.

A hut, with open sides and a grass-covered roof, was used by the Caddo in summer. It had a latticework platform, woven with twigs fastened to a framework that was set two feet off the ground.

The Choctaw Indians, who lived in southern and central Mississippi, were excellent farmers. They built large villages which contained special huts to store their crops of corn. Choctaw dwellings were completely covered with the large leaves of the palmetto tree.

Indian clans, living in eastern North Carolina, built bark-covered wigwams. Frames were made of pine, cedar, or hickory poles and covered with cypress or cedar bark which was warmed in a fire to make it tough. While warm, the bark was bent into place. Smaller poles were placed in the ground over the bark strips to hold them firmly in place. Pine bark, reed mats, or skins were sometimes used in the same manner. These homes had fires in the middle of the floor under a small smoke hole. Benches, built around the interior wall, were covered with woven mats and animal hides.

Most of the larger Carolina Indian villages had council houses in their center. These were built in the same manner as the family dwellings, but on a much larger scale. Used for ceremonial purposes, they were often built on top of earthen mounds.

The frameworks of Cherokee dwellings were made of large, upright posts set in the ground two or three feet apart. Smaller posts were placed in between the posts, making a basket-like wall. Grass was then mixed with smooth earth or clay and plastered over the wall. This is called wattle-and-daub construction. The roof was covered with bark and then thatched with grass. The inside of the dwelling contained a fireplace in its center; a hole in the roof allowed smoke to escape.

Beds were raised off the ground on short posts. Hemlock boughs, broom sage, and other similar materials were placed under the woven mats of the bed frames.

Perhaps the most popular image of the Southeastern Indian is the Seminole of Florida. Their stately dwellings, with open sides and thatched roofs, remained long into the eighteenth century.

The southern third of the Florida peninsula has a tropical climate. The rest of the state is semi-tropical, with hot, moist weather in summer and mild weather in winter. Florida's cli-

Cherokee dwelling.

mate is due to the North Equatorial Current, or Gulf Stream, a river of warm water which circles clockwise in the Atlantic between North America and Europe. In some places, this current is nearly 100 miles wide. Flowing between Cuba and Florida, it passes near the Keys and creates a tropical climate as far north as Palm Beach.

Each Seminole village had two separate houses about twenty yards apart. One dwelling was 30 feet long by 12 feet wide. It was divided into two rooms—one for cooking and the other for sleeping. The second dwelling was about the same size as the first, but was two stories high. A shaded, raised platform at one end was adjacent to the front door and was reached by a portable ladder. This was where the head of the family received visitors and found comfort during the hot weather.

The dwellings were constructed of heavy timbers placed in the ground at four corners, with lighter beams along the sides

Seminole village.

and cross-pieces to strengthen the walls. The sides were left open, and the roof was covered with a thatch of reed, grass, or palm leaves. The floor was raised off the ground for protection from seasonal rains. Cypress, which is very durable, and cane were used for the framework.

Each family had an individual garden near their own dwelling, but two miles from a village was a common garden that was planted and maintained by the entire village. The gardens were usually fenced or palisaded with cane sticks or other timbers placed in the ground.

DWELLING MATERIALS

Cabbage Palmetto

(Sabal palmetto)

The long leaves of the palmetto were used by the Indians of the Southeast to thatch their dwellings. Cabbage palmetto may be found in sandy soils along the Gulf Coast and on the west coast of the Florida peninsula.

Cabbage palmetto (*sabal palmetto*).

The palmetto reaches a height of 80 feet. The base of the tree is straight, while the upper portion is covered with broad leaves. The leaves are long, firm, wedge-shaped at the base, and quite thick. Dark green in color, they grow from five to six feet in length and sometimes as broad as eight feet. The fruit of the palmetto ripens in the autumn. It is one-third of an inch in diameter, and has a seed which is covered with a thick, sweet fruit. Palmetto wood is light and soft.

Bald Cypress

(Taxodium distichum)

Anyone familiar with a southern swampland knows the characteristic appearance of a bald cypress swamp. To those in other parts of the country, it conjures up images of crocodiles and eerie clusters of mangroves.

Along the humid coasts, bald cypress trunks are often draped with Spanish moss. The tree is all that remains of a similar, but ancient, species that was once distributed over North America and northern Europe. The bald cypress is as much at home on land as in the water. However, it is most common in lowlands that are under water most of the year. Bald cypress may be found from the coast of southern Delaware to southern Florida, the Gulf Coast of Texas, and along the river valleys of southern Illinois and southwestern Indiana.

Although bald cypress looks like an evergreen tree, it is a deciduous tree that loses its leaves in the fall. The leaves are flat and about one-quarter to one-half inches long. They are light yellow-green, and have a feathery appearance. When they drop in the fall, they are yellow or brown.

Both the male and female flowers of the tree develop on the twigs of the preceding year's growth. Male flowers are purplish and are borne in clusters, while the female flowers are scattered near the ends of the branchlets. It takes only a single season for

Bald cypress (*taxodium distichum*).

the female blooms to develop into tiny, one-inch purplish cones. Bald cypress bark is reddish-brown. It is ridged on old trees, but only slightly ridged on younger trees. The "knees," or roots, which rise out of the water, are hollow and covered with bark. These roots help anchor the tree to the unstable soils of the swamp.

It is easy to see why the Indians of the Southwest preferred this wood to many others when building their homes. It is very durable in contact with the soil, and so resistant to adverse weather that it is often referred to as "the wood eternal."

HOW TO BUILD A SEMINOLE SHELTER

Materials

1 Twin-sized bedsheet (72" x 100")
2 4' forked palmetto timbers
4 4' straight palmetto timbers
1 9' straight palmetto timber
Hand trowel
Twine
Scissors
Needle and heavy-duty thread

The Seminole, like many other tribes of North America, left their permanent home sites at various seasons to hunt and gather wild foods. They built several types of temporary shelters at these camp sites. One kind was constructed much like their permanent dwelling, with palmetto timbers for framing and palmetto leaves for the roof. Because the temporary shelter was used for a short period of time, it was erected on dry land and did not need a platform for protection from high water. The shelters were built more for protection from the hot summer sun. It is possible to build a small Seminole-type summer shelter with palmetto timbers and a bedsheet.

1. Locate a twin-sized bedsheet. It will measure 72" x 100". Make a small hole in each of the four corners of the sheet and sew an overcast stitch around the edge of the holes (A).
2. Locate palmetto timbers for the frame. You will need two 4' timbers that are forked at one end, four 4' straight timbers, and one 9' straight timber.
3. Dig a hole in the ground six inches deep and set one of the forked timbers in the hole (B).

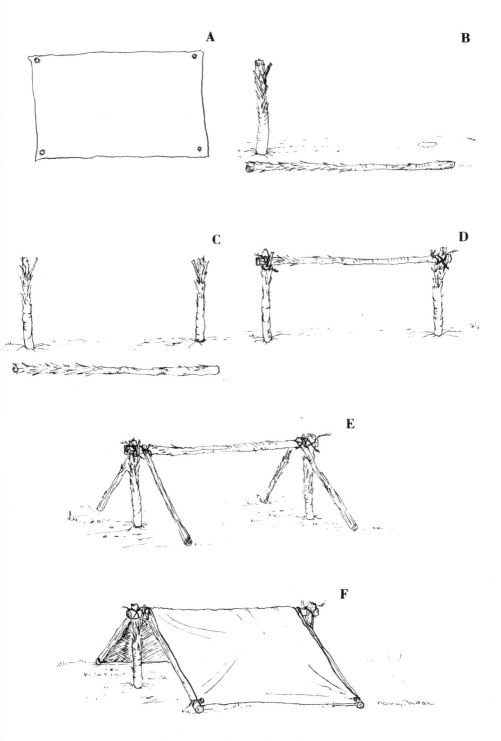

How to build a Seminole shelter.

4. Place the 9' timber on the ground with one end extending four inches beyond the upright timber. Dig a second hole four inches in from the other end of the 9' timber (B).
5. Place the second forked 4' timber in the hole and pack the earth down around it (C).
6. Place the ridgepole across the forked timbers and lash it in place (D).
7. Place the four remaining timbers behind the forked upright timbers, leaning them against the ridgepole (E). (It is a good idea to lash these in place with strong twine.)
8. Place the sheet over the ridgepole. Tie it down at all four corners (F).

NORTHEAST

The Indians of the Northeast are often referred to as the Woodland Indians because the same area that was once ice and tundra later became lush, deciduous forests, and grassy, open areas, and fresh- and salt-water marshes. The trees in the forests were the source of many of the building materials of many tribes.

Fresh-water estuaries in the region produced many species of fish and shellfish, and a variety of grapes, strawberries, plums, and blueberries grew in the rich soils along the coast and in the valleys.

The low, relatively flat land of eastern North America allows the summer winds to carry moisture into the central portion of the area. This yearly source of rain once encouraged forest

Algonkian village.

growth, which in turn produced an abundance of berries, nuts, and plants. These resources in turn made the territory an especially good hunting ground.

The tribes of the Northeast lived from Canada to Virginia and from the confluence of the Illinois and Ohio Rivers to the Atlantic coast. They were skilled fishermen, farmers, hunters, and wild-food gatherers. Around the Great Lakes, the Indians caught muskellunge and landlocked salmon. Along the coastal areas, they collected mussels, clams, crabs, and oysters, which they smoked and stored for winter.

The Algonkian tribes lived in small, independent villages in large, dome-shaped wigwams covered with bark or mats woven of cattails. A single wigwam held about 10 people, and a typical village contained two or three wigwams. The Algonkians planted crops of corn, beans, and squash in the spring. In summer, they fished in the rivers and streams between the mountains and coast.

The Central Algonkians who lived in the forests around the Great Lakes, consisted of the Menomini, Potawatomi, Ottawa, and Chippewa Tribes. Within the Central Algonkian territory were the Prairie tribes: Sauk, Fox, Kickapoo, Miami, Peoria, Illinois, Shawnee, Piankashaw, Prairie, and Winnebago.

Most Central Algonkian tribes built large, dome-shaped wigwams, made by placing saplings in the ground, bending them at the top, and tying them together. Additional saplings were tied on horizontally, and the whole frame was covered with those materials most readily available in the area. For example, the Chippewa in the north used white birch bark to cover their

Chippewa birch-bark wigwams.

Kickapoo bark house and storage platform.

wigwams. They were able to secure twenty-foot rolls of bark in spring when the sap started to flow. The bark was placed around the outside of a wigwam, from the bottom up. It was made to overlap in the same manner we overlap shingles on our homes. Additional saplings were laid over the bark to hold it down. The wigwams had interior benches and sleeping platforms. The Chippewa also built a bark-covered tipi, which they used in summer when they went on fishing and hunting expeditions.

Wigwams in the region of what is now Minnesota were made of mats woven of rushes. Further south, the Kickapoo built large, bark dwellings with poles on the outside to hold the bark in place.

South of the Great Lakes, where the forests blended into the prairie, some tribes used grass to cover their dome-shaped wigwams.

The Eastern Algonkian Indians lived along the Atlantic coast and as far inland as the Connecticut River Valley. Among the tribes were the Micmac, Malecite, Pennacook, Mohican,

Pequot, Massachusetts, Montauk, Abnaki, Narragansett, Wampanoag, and Delaware.

The hardwood forests of the area contained trees with wood that was impossible to cut without tools. Thus, the Eastern Algonkian used only young, flexible saplings to frame their bark-covered dwellings. Because birch tree growth was scarce below southern Maine, the Indians used elm, hickory, or ash bark for their wigwams. Where bark was not available, they wove coverings out of cattails and grasses.

The Iroquois lived in the region between the central and eastern Algonkian territory. Iroquois tribes included the Mohawk, who lived along the Hudson River in New York; the Oneida, Onodaga, Cayuga, and Seneca, who lived west of the Mohawk; the Huron, who lived around Lake Ontario; and the Neutral, who lived in the areas along Lake Erie.

The Iroquois lived in large, palisaded villages, built on flat land beside rivers or lakes. Outside of the villages, the Iroquois cultivated large crops of corn, beans, or squash. A typical Iroquois village consisted of a group of rectangular long houses,

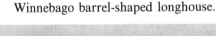

Winnebago barrel-shaped longhouse.

each holding about ten families. Some long houses were built by placing two long rows of saplings in the ground, bending them at the top, and tying them together. One of the most common coverings for the long house was elm bark. When elm was not available, the bark of other trees was used.

DWELLING MATERIALS

Red Maple

(Acer rubrum)

The Indians of the Northeast had a number of deciduous trees to choose from when building their wigwams. The red

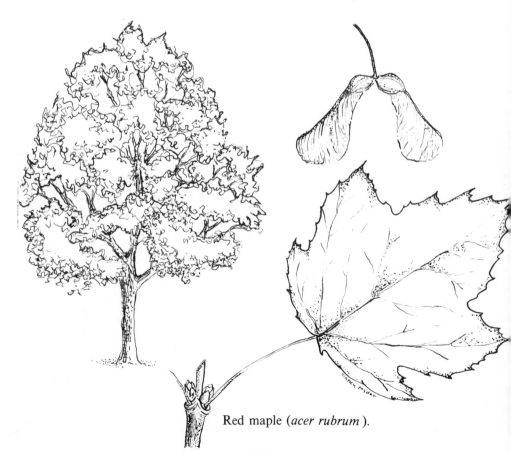

Red maple (*acer rubrum*).

maple was valued for its great flexibility and abundance. Swamp white oak and other saplings were also used.

In a red maple forest, many young saplings spring up and become so numerous that not all reach maturity. Judicious pruning promotes healthy growth in the forest. The red maple grows in wet areas and on hillsides with moist soil. It frequently is referred to as swamp maple because it can stand in water for an extended period of time and still remain alive. One reason it is referred to as a red maple is because it is the first tree to turn red in the fall; in the spring, clusters of bright yellow or red flowers burst forth ahead of the leaves. In winter, identification can be made by looking for the fat red buds on the end of the tree's red twigs. The bark of a young tree is silvery gray, but when mature it turns dark brown and becomes shaggy.

The red maple has leaves with three to five lobes. The buds and leaves grow opposite each other on the branch. (Four of the most common woodland trees with buds and leaves arranged opposite each other are: maple, ash, dogwood, and horse-chestnut.)

Cattail

(Typha latifolia)

Cattails were one of the favorite weaving materials of many tribes because the plants could usually be found in marshlands. The narrow-leaved cattail is scarcer in the east than in California and other parts of the Pacific Coast. The Indians of the Northeast used cattails to weave durable, waterproof mats with which they covered their wigwams. The dried leaves were so strong that European settlers used them for rush seating on chairs.

Cattails grow along the banks of rivers and streams and on the banks of ponds and lakes. In the Northeast, they are predominant in the marshes of the areas where spring rains and

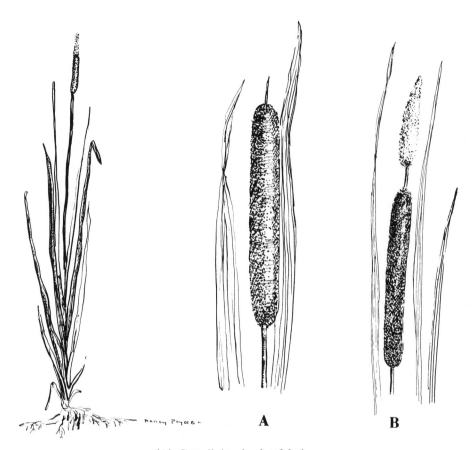

(A) Cattail (*typha latifolia*).
(B) Narrow-leaved cattail (*typha anqustifolia*).

melting snows are held until they run off to the sea or become absorbed in the earth.

A cattail marsh has a very characteristic appearance. It is an area where trees do not grow because the ground is too wet. In summer, the marshes will be painted green with mature cattail plants. In winter, before the snow falls, an entire marsh will be filled with brown cattails.

Cattail leaves are ribbon-shaped, the common cattail having a leaf almost an inch wide. The inside of the leaf is filled with large air holes, which makes it shrink when it dries. The tall, brown flowering spike of the cattail appears in early summer. The bright yellow pollen at the top of the spike was used by the Indians to make flour. The flowering spike, when mature, was used to insulate homes.

The rootstock of the cattail, which is under water, branches sideways and grows two to three inches thick. Cattails can be collected in late fall by cutting them at the base. Pulling them up destroys their root system. The cut leaves should be tied in bundles and dried in the sun. When they are thoroughly dry, they can be used for weaving.

HOW TO BUILD A WIGWAM

Materials

8	10' saplings
12 to 20	5' saplings
1	8' branch
1	16" stake
	Twine
	Hand Trowel, or pointed shovel
2	Medium-sized rocks (for cutting)

Note: Instead of using scissors to cut twine, place the twine on a stone and give it a hard whack with another stone. This will cut it very quickly.

You will have to locate saplings or branches before construction begins. It is a good idea to measure the size of your saplings by standing beside them with your arm extended straight up. If the tree is about double this height, it will be adequate. Use a small handsaw or try cutting the tree down with a sharp stone.

Cutting twine with stones.

Establishing a fixed point.

Notched stake in place. First two saplings in ground.

The saplings should be pruned in the woods to make them easier to transport. Also, cut branches left in the forest can be used by small animals for their homes and shelters.

Indian habitats were built in circles, ovals, and rectangles. Although dwellings were symmetrical and very well proportioned, the Indians did not have a unit of measure, nor did they know how to use the plumb line or T square. Thus, it is fun to discover ways the Indians might have laid out a circle. Here is one way to do it:

1. Locate a fairly straight 8′ branch and notch it in the middle.
2. Drive a small stake all the way into the ground. This will guarantee a permanent fixed point.
3. Place the notch on the branch directly over the stake.
4. Dig a hole and put a sapling at least six inches into the ground at either end of the pole on the ground.

93

Lashing saplings together.

5. Keep the notch on the pole over the stake and rotate the branch, cutting the circle roughly in half, then in quarters, then in eighths.

6. As the saplings are put into the ground, arch them overhead and lash them together with strong twine. (They should overlap at the top for lashing.) For a wigwam 8′ in diameter, eight saplings, each about 10′ tall, are enough, although more will add to the wigwam's stability.

7. Lash the smaller saplings, about 5′ long, around the

Lashing horizontal saplings to frame.

Tying on mats.

structure horizontally. They should be put on at about one-foot intervals from bottom to top.

8. Tie on woven mats, bundles of grass, or similar materials.

9. Leave a hole in the top for smoke and an opening toward the east or south for a door.

SELECTED BIBLIOGRAPHY

Albrectsen, Lis. *Teepee and Moccasin: Indian Craft for Young People.* New York: Van Nostrand Reinhold Co., 1972.

Bjorklund, Karna L. *The Indians of Northeastern America.* New York: Dodd, Mead Co., 1969.

Bleeker, Sonia. *The Chippewa Indians: Rice Gatherers of the Great Lakes.* New York: William Morrow Co., Inc., 1955.

Brown, Vinson. *Peoples of the Sea Wind.* New York: Macmillan Publishing Co., 1977.

Catlin, George. *Letters and Notes on the Manners, Customs and Conditions of the North American Indians.* 2 vols. New York: Dover Publications, Inc., 1967.

Chalfant, Stuart A. *Nez Percé Indians, Aboriginal Territory of the Nez Percé Indians.* New York: Garland Publishing, Inc., 1974.

Collingwood, G.H., and Warren D. Brush. *Knowing Your Trees.* Washington, D.C.: The American Forestry Association, 1964.

Doster, James F. *The Creek Indians and Their Florida Lands.* 2 vols. New York: Garland Publishing, Inc., 1974.

Dozier, Edward P. *The Pueblo Indians of North America.* New York: Holt, Rinehart and Winston, Inc., 1970.

Driver, Harold E. *Indians of North America.* Chicago: University of Chicago Press, 1972.

Drucker, Philip. *Indians of the Northwest Coast.* Garden City, New York: Natural History Press, 1955.

Heizer, Robert F., and M.A. Whipple, eds. *The California Indians: A Source Book.* Berkeley: University of California Press, 1971.

Hodge, Frederick Webb. *Handbook of American Indians North of Mexico.* Washington, D.C.: Smithsonian Institute, Bureau of Ethnology Bulletin #30, 2 vols., 1907–1910.

Horr, David Agee, ed. *American Indian Ethnohistory: California and Basin-Plateau Indians.* Waltham, Mass.: Brandeis University, undated. Reprinted, New York: Garland Publishing, Inc., 1974.

Hudson, Charles M. *Four Centuries of Southern Indians.* Athens: The University of Georgia Press, 1965.

Kroeber, A.L. *Handbook of the Indians of California.* New York: Dover Publications, Inc., 1976.

———, and T.T. Waterman. *Source Book in Anthropology.* New York: Harcourt, Brace and Co., 1931.

Morgan, Lewis H. *Houses and House Life of the American Aborigines.* Chicago: University of Chicago Press, 1965.

Murdock, George Peter. *Plateau Culture and Society.* Pittsburgh: University of Pittsburgh Press, 1965.

National Geographic Book Service. *Our Continent.* Washington, D.C.: National Geographic Society, 1976.

———. *The World of the American Indian.* Washington, D.C.: National Geographic Society, 1974.

Palmer, E. Lawrence. *Fieldbook of Natural History.* New York: McGraw-Hill Book Company, 1949.

Seton, Julia M. *American Indian Arts: A Way of Life.* New York: The Ronald Press Co., 1962.

Underhill, Ruth M. *Indians of the Pacific Northwest.* Washington, D.C.: U.S. Department of the Interior, Branch of Education, 1945.

———. *First Penthouse Dwellers of America.* Santa Fe: Laboratory of Anthropology, 1946.

———. *People of the Crimson Evening.* Washington, D.C.: U.S. Department of the Interior, Bureau of Indian Affairs, Branch of Education, 1951.

Waterman, T.T. "North American Indian Dwellings." *The Geographical Review,* Vol. XIV (January, 1924), No. 1.

COMMON METRIC EQUIVALENTS AND CONVERSIONS

Approximate

1 inch	= 25 millimeters
1 foot	= 0.3 meter
1 yard	= 0.9 meter
1 square inch	= 6.5 square centimeters
1 square foot	= 0.09 square meter
1 square yard	= 0.8 square meter
1 millimeter	= 0.04 inch
1 meter	= 3.3 feet
1 meter	= 1.1 yards
1 square centimeter	= 0.16 square inch

Accurate to Parts Per Million

inches × 25.4°	= millimeters
feet × 0.3048°	= meters
yards × 0.9144°	= meters
square inches × 6.4516°	= square centimeters
square feet × 0.092903	= square meters
square yards × 0.836127	= square meters

INDEX